YOU CAN DO IT!

Gymnastics

Kirk Bizley

To Natasha, Jason, Sarah and Dean

First published in Great Britain by Heinemann Library
Halley Court, Jordan Hill, Oxford OX2 8EJ
a division of Reed Educational and Professional Publishing Ltd.
Heinemann is a registered trademark of Reed Educational & Professional Publishing Limited.

OXFORD MELBOURNE AUCKLAND IBADAN JOHANNESBURG
BLANTYRE GABORONE PORTSMOUTH (NH) USA CHICAGO

Designed by Ken Vail Graphic Design, Cambridge
Illustrations by Graham-Cameron Illustration (Susan Hutchinson)
Originated by Ambassador Litho Ltd
Printed by Wing King Tong in Hong Kong

03 02 01 00 99
10 9 8 7 6 5 4 3 2 1

ISBN 0 431 08530 7

British Library Cataloguing in Publication Data

Bizley, Kirk
Gymnastics. – (You can do it)
1. Gymnastics – Juvenile literature
I. Title
796.4'4

Acknowledgements
The author would like to thank the staff and pupils of Shepton Mallett Community Infants School.

The Publishers would like to thank the following for permission to reproduce photographs:
Trevor Clifford, pages 4, 5, 6, 8, 10, 12, 14, 19, 21; Empics, page 16.

Cover photograph reproduced with permission of John Walmsley

Our thanks to Betty Root for her comments in the preparation of this book.

Every effort has been made to contact copyright holders of any material reproduced in this book.
Any omissions will be rectified in subsequent printings if notice is given to the Publisher.

For more information about Heinemann Library books, or to order, please phone 01865 888066,
or send a fax to 01865 314091. You can visit our web site at www.heinemann.co.uk

Contents

Words in bold letters **like these** are explained in the Glossary.

What do you need?

You need three things for gymnastics.

1 The right clothes.

2 The proper place to work in.

3 The right equipment.

These two children are wearing the right sort of clothing.

Some shorts and a T-shirt are fine for boys.

Girls can wear the same, or maybe a **leotard**.

You can have bare feet. But if the floor is rough, you should wear trainers.

There are lots of different kinds of equipment you can use in gymnastics. This equipment is called **apparatus**.

Some of this is shown in the picture, and you may be allowed to use it. Only use it if a grown-up is with you.

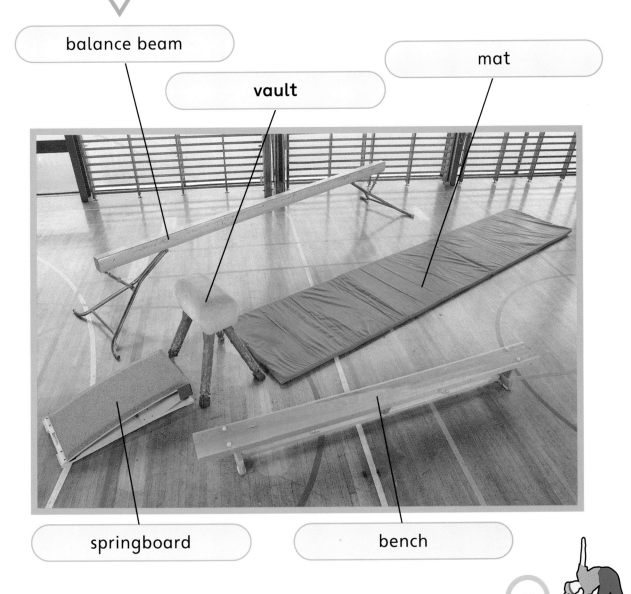

balance beam

vault

mat

springboard

bench

Are you ready?

Before you do gymnastics, make sure your body is ready. This is called a **warm-up**. It helps you to do better. It also helps to make sure that you do not hurt yourself!

Start with a little run. Or you can just run on the spot, or do some skipping.

Now you need to get your **muscles** warmed up. The best way is to move your **joints** – your shoulders, elbows, knees and waist.

Try some **stretching** exercises too. These make your muscles warmer and more stretchy so they can move as much as possible.

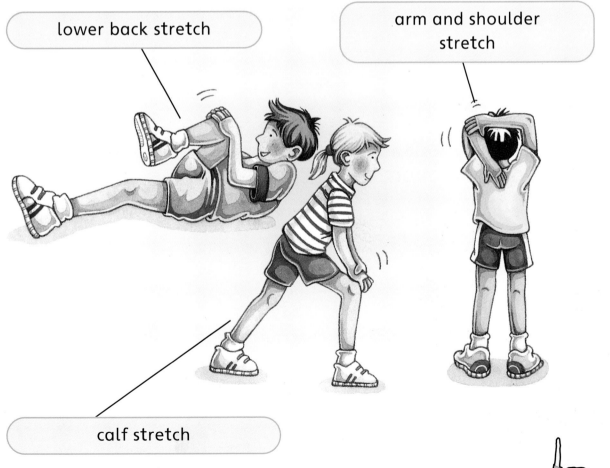

lower back stretch

arm and shoulder stretch

calf stretch

Are you in shape?

Being able to bend your body easily means that you can make different shapes with your body.

You can make long, straight shapes.

You can make small, curled-up shapes.

Try making your own long and small shapes.

You can make other shapes, too. You need to support yourself in different ways and move your body in different directions.

You can support yourself on your front.

Or you can support yourself on your back.

You can make other shapes if you support your body. Here is a more difficult one!

Working together

A great thing about gymnastics is that you can do it with your friends.

Try playing 'follow the leader'. If one of you does something, the other one has to copy it.

Or try doing the same thing at the same time.

With a friend you can also help each other to do some difficult things. If you cannot do a balance on your own, perhaps your friend can help you.

SAFETY STAR
Never try to support a friend in a very difficult movement. They might get hurt!

You can work back to back. You can also face your friend and do the same thing. This is like you being a mirror. It takes a lot of practise!

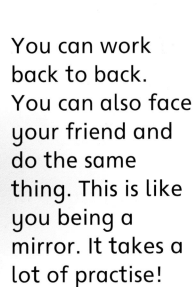

Let's move!

One of the best things in gymnastics is putting all your movements together. This is called a **routine.**

Let's look at the different ways you can move.

You can walk.   You can hop.   You can even skip.

Always try to make all your movements as neat and smooth as possible. Try to look good!

You can work out your own movements to move from one shape to another.

You don't have to stand up, you can just change the position of your body.

You could go from this…　　　…to this…

…just by moving your arms and body.

Or you could go from this…　…to this

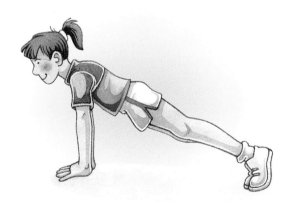 

…just by moving your legs.

You can make these movements backwards and forwards. You can add even more to your routine.

Rolling around

A fun way to move around is to roll your body. You can move forwards, backwards and sideways like this.

Start with this **roll**. Just lie down on your back, bring your knees up, then rock backwards and forwards.

This is a long sideways roll, or a log roll. Start from your long, straight shape. Then roll over onto your tummy.

SAFETY STAR
Don't try difficult rolls until you are sure you can do the easy ones.

For the basic roll, lie on the end of a **bench** or a **box** top. Move forward off the edge, so you can rest your hands on the mat. Slowly push yourself forwards and curl your body up so you can roll over.

For the tin soldier roll, sit down with your legs apart and straight. Hold your legs just below your knees. Now roll around on your shoulders and the middle of your back.

Now you have some rolls to add to your **routine**.

On the ground

Floorwork is when you do lots of different movements on the **mats**. This is when you can put together all the things you have learnt!

You need to get a lot of mats together so you have enough room to do your **routine**.

Try moving from one shape to another, especially when you need to stand up.

A forward **roll** is another great movement.

1 Start off like this.

2 Put your hands down. Tuck your head closely in. Push yourself off and forwards.

3 Let your bottom go over your head. Keep your legs bent. Push with your hands.

4 Try to roll forward so you end up back in your starting position.

SAFETY STAR
Never roll on your head in a forward roll. Use your hands and shoulders.

Ready for take-off?

These are some of the shapes you can make when you jump in the air.

This is called a **tuck** shape. Bring your knees up as far as they will go. Try not to drop your head down.

This is a star shape. Try to get your legs and arms as far apart as you can.

SAFETY STAR
Ask a grown-up to help when you make these shapes. Always have thick, soft **mats** to land on.

These things can help you jump higher.

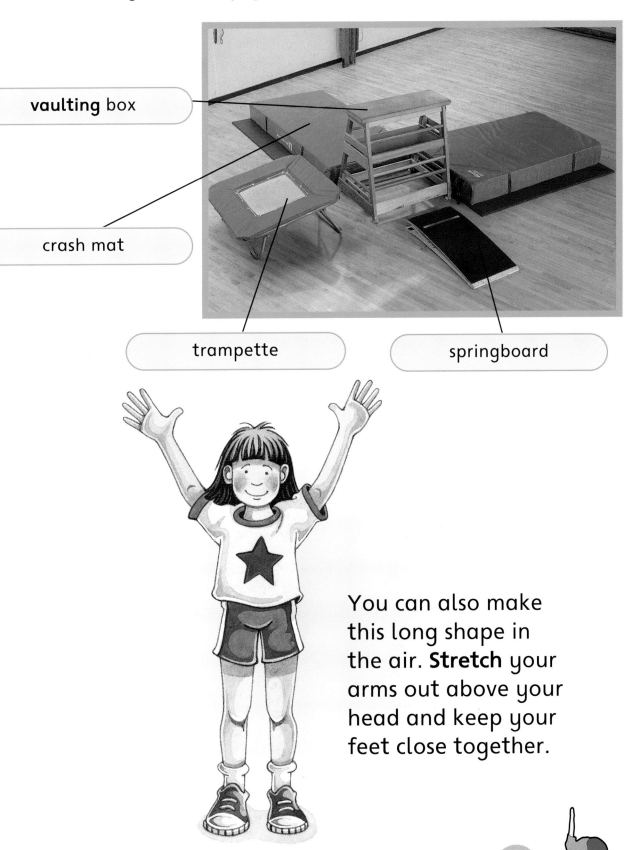

vaulting box

crash mat

trampette

springboard

You can also make this long shape in the air. **Stretch** your arms out above your head and keep your feet close together.

Up and away!

Vaulting is when you jump onto something, or over it.

For an easy vault just run up to the **box** and jump on.

Now walk to the end and jump off. You can make one of your favourite shapes in the air before you land on the **mat!**

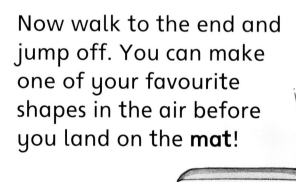

For a side vault you need some of the other **apparatus**. You are going to go right over the box!

You need to use your **tuck** shape for this vault.

Safety

There are safety stars all through this book. Read all of them!

Here are all the safety rules.

Equipment

Equipment must only be moved and put out by grown-ups.

There must be lots of room between the equipment.

There must be plenty of **mats**. There should not be gaps between the mats.

The floor must be clean and not slippery. Wear trainers if a floor is rough.

Look out for all these things! Tell a grown-up if they are not right!

Grown-ups

You must always have a grown-up with you.

Only do things which the grown-up tells you to do. Make sure you try to do them properly.

Be sensible all the time. You do not want to hurt yourself, or anyone else!

Safety for you

Make sure you are dressed properly for gymnastics.

Have a proper **warm-up** to get you ready.

Cool-down!

When you have finished, you must have a **cool-down**. This is to let your body get back to normal after all the work it has done.

A simple cool-down is to do all the things you did in your warm-up again. But do fewer of them and for less time.

If you follow all these rules, you will enjoy yourself and be safe. Remember,

YOU CAN DO IT!

Glossary

apparatus equipment used for gymnastics

balance beam narrow bar to balance on

bench long wooden piece of equipment

box piece of equipment you use to vault on and over

cool-down way of moving to relax your body after exercise

floorwork movements done on mats

joint place where your bones meet and you can bend, like your shoulders and knees

leotard one-piece costume worn for gymnastics

mat padded area to do exercises on

muscle part of your body which helps you bend and stretch

roll movements done by twisting or turning your body around sideways, forwards or backwards

routine group of movements put together in a row

springboard equipment which helps you jump higher

stretching moving your muscles at the joints as much as you can

trampette mini-trampoline which helps you jump higher

tuck shape made when you are in the air and bring your knees in to, and up to, your chest

vault/vaulting jumping over something. Also the name of the equipment you jump over.

warm-up way of moving to get your body ready for exercise

Index